GIVERS
&
TAKERS

POEMS BY

Jane Mayhall

THE EAKINS PRESS
NEW YORK

COPYRIGHT © 1968 JANE MAYHALL
Library of Congress Catalog Number 68-55445
'The Marshes' and 'Chanson Malaise' appeared in *The Quarterly Review of Literature*, 'Mozart' in *The New York Times*, and 'November 1963,' 'The Confinement' and 'The Builder' in *East Image*.

CONTENTS

Ode to a Snack Watcher 5
New Movies 6
Yeah for Multi Media 7
A Visit to the Rich 8
The Day After Dr. King 9
Sell-Out (for Percussion) 10
Chanson Malaise 12
Backwards to Progress 13
For a Cracked Glass Window 14
The Confinement 16
Portrait d'une Femme 18
On the Misuses of Freud 19
Notes for That Big Gold Book 20
The Marshes 22
At Ayot St. Lawrence 24
To Hobbema 26

Franz Schubert 28
For the Market 31
The Subway Church 32
On First Hearing Berlioz 34
Mozart 35
JFK 36
Matter and Reality 37
W. W. Plaza 38
November 1963 39
The Builder 40
Givers & Takers 42
Beyond Hysteria 43
Ideas Are For Use 44
Is? 45
The Instrument 46

ODE TO A SNACK WATCHER

Idleness! your spit is a murderer.
Your passivity makes you vicious.
You are that melancholy crotch of
                    television
that drives the young to fawn
like imbeciles on machines
and adults to whine and stuff their guts,
like sick-bed louts, with poison.
Sloth is your only name,
mass-culture, drenched with crime.
"But people want it!"
the polls all say.
Nightmares to keep them on smiling.

NEW MOVIES

With the great effulgence
of grammatical impossibility,
this is syrup, not blood;
corpses are run-over dolls;
big lights that offer us blindness;
mediocrity doting on monsters.
Our culture, like Peter,
makes us deny ourselves.
Even consequences are borrowed,
in these starved, salacious plays;
paranoic dreams that feed
on hearsay lies.

YEAH FOR MULTI MEDIA

It's living in a small room with small brains;
the only way to be heard is to be unpleasant.
Then they rave as if you'd said something
                              gorgeous.
I hate to imply, maybe Hitler won the war.
The movies advertise themselves as horror. Dumb
girls oscillating in pink mink: "I *mean*, you'll love
it. It's sadistic!" Set-faced children with clocks in
their heads; and teen-agers acting like secret police,
burning up books and ideas. "But young
                              people are
always fascistic!" Yeah. Old/young, influence,
contamination. The fictive flash of nothing.

Maybe we're only getting the scum, that rises to
the top. And underneath, the green imports are
                              nascent.

A VISIT TO THE RICH

Money is
the epitome of dung.
Vegetable, or human?
I don't mean to
talk against it;
only, understand.

THE DAY AFTER DR. KING

TODAY, there were more people in the library than in the department stores. A clear sky, nothing strange. But even the word "department" seems, if not important, transgressing by its overwrought confusions. His love was an evaluation. And a library is not a briar of lies. Here, derivations shift and go not asunder. But no day like today, and none will ever be. Despair has launched us onto another plane. And to be confused is not confusing. We must educate for what he was doing. To bring him back to us, who will never return.

SELL-OUT (FOR PERCUSSION)

Shock appeal. Shock shock shock
knock knock knock knock where's Bach?
Not. Reduce yourself to illiteracy,
(illegibility) ill ill anything
and you are saying something
SUPPOSED to be. Advertising,
they are all advertising, you are
all advertising. Nothing is anything
UNLESS. Is this because why?
Intelligence is tension, dimension,
extension. Children are fed
pap so then aptly are poets, dressed in
ice-cream candy-coated pills of
("ick") dull philosophy. Not sugar candy
but but but what? Is this because
WHY? Distress is the new sweet
gooey, chewy, yum-yummy, everybody

rolling in molasses of ouch help
SELF-CONSCIENCE-lessness. Don't
think just yell in the loudest voice
possible. Shock knock flock
to electronic mock sock lock;
dish out the deal, cook
it in garbage. All that you
feel, translate into outrage.
Fake madman, pietistic, slick.

CHANSON MALAISE

The old-heads are drinking;
the new-heads are junking;
quick, quick, quack, quack,
who is thinking?

The cash is consistent,
the cliché rewarding;
we live in good times
of honest retarding.

What's left to blame
if murderers seem cute?
When everybody laughs
it must be a joke.

BACKWARDS TO PROGRESS

To be alive is a prayer.
You say god does not exist;
your folly, my snare.
It is either a tired
relation, or an over-
zealous interpreting.
But when the days drag,
they are maneuvering us
to care.

FOR A CRACKED GLASS WINDOW

Though I speak with the lungs
of mammon and bangles
and have not clarity
I am become as the sounding ass,

or a shrinking symbol,
and though I make
short shrift of competency
and understand

all the miseries
and all follies,
and though I have wrath
and could consume

nations, and have
not clarity,
I am shamming.
And though I have the gift

for contingency,
and crises to come,
bestrewing my blood
for the greed of the more,

and though I give
my hackles to be spurned,
and have not clarity,
it drops into feigning.

THE CONFINEMENT

An irritant, sticking pins of beatle-music
into his thorny-skinned self,
he sat, half-sliding off the seat of the bus,
the transistor clapped to his long-skulled head
and spread out his skinny legs (which held
a fat-wrapped package for NBC).
Nobody would sit next to him,
the pustulate white and ravaged flesh,
and a pink-faced homosexual motioned me
graciously to the seat. I took the
offering. Scurries of crazed jerkings
and a miasma of uncontrolled winkings
wracked his music-starved overcoat,
and I felt god don't let this misery
touch me. But I didn't move aside
(who for? god? god, for you? god?)
so that, though it wasn't my
doing, at Twenty-Third Street

he knew enough to turn off the dial,
get to his feet and walk straight
to the bus door,
and find his way out.

PORTRAIT D'UNE FEMME

She communicates by accusation.
Her effect on friends is, at best,
a laxative. She irritates or purges.
If your mentality is in good order,
you only get indigestion.
That is the worst, maybe.
You develop stoic forces
that can be interpreted by yourself
as useful bits of grit
to secretly spur or hinder
the tides of sanguine judgement.
She may be superficial or deep,
according to what connects;
but not necessarily part of the
                             human condition.
And her malice defies index.

ON THE MISUSES OF FREUD

There are enough psychiatrist jokes
to fill the buckets of the Poor March,
but the evasions persist.
Middle-aged coupon clippers,
with Fifth Avenue *dégagé* coiffures,
still take their ravaged faces
to the couch.
Help me, they cry, licking
their wounds like chocolate;
and the humble walk by
(mute step)
praying for a cure.

NOTES FOR THAT BIG GOLD BOOK

All evaporated, nobody real.
Yesterday was not so much better.
Then, I didn't try or exert.
When the good-looking couple
made nasty fun of cripples,
I thought, "oh well, the sins
of the world." I was an easy-going
snob. And the couple seemed to me
no more capable than worms.
I know now, they rule the ramparts
of the sky.

To evaporate is to die.
The standards are collapsed.
Jiggling puppets of wickedness
flay their victims, victims
flay their gods.

We are dawdling and obscene,
slaves to catastrophism.
(Nothing was intrinsic but desire.)
What is the difference to me?
My muscles ache like foam
bristling on the waters. Disillusion,
emptiness conjoin.

But I feel a raging impulse:
"Listen to me, world. *Now* you
must change."

THE MARSHES

All that running water outside;
the running faces, the rocks of blood,
the melting waste that tangles the bushes;
a strong wind blows, and I will not
                        subvert course.
Blocks of people with hysterical blotches
are rushing past, whirling on their big
television teeth gutturals and maxims.
I knew them before, they were numbers and
mewling crowds, that tangled up
                        our thoughts
among the weeds.

For every clear idea, the marsh is
                        sucking through;
glutted human thrall, majorities
                        and gurgles.

Oily bubbles wrangle out their wars.
How can I keep my course?
                    Chekov, Mozart,
imagining in your mind
lives of discipline and drain,
through whose filaments
the marshes run.

AT AYOT ST. LAWRENCE

(*Home of G. B. Shaw*)

It bothers them to look at you, Shaw.
Your cold calculations rake
their nerve streams, like sons of
                            holy orphans.
"We are burning up inside," they quote
their quotable passion.
You are a general parent,
a parent generalization.

It hurts them to love your kind of hate,
"*Widower's Houses*," clear depiction of a state;
as, on your piano, still, an opened page
                            of Bach.
Your big hat is hanging on the rack.
Brains! you said. Brains, not madness.
And, "Intellectual courtesy,
and serious consideration. . ."

Whether you meant it or not,
that was years before you died.
History has turned another block.
They are afraid, and dare not sanity:
"Who needs it? Too much work!"

TO HOBBEMA

(Dutch painter, 1638–1709)

The shadow has just fallen
over your road (my road)
and the cricket outside
my window tugs at your
red thatch. But I am your crooked
tree, set to mark a cloud. I am
that violent. Yesterday, I
saw two boys in New York
beat a geranium plant with an
iron pipe. They killed it.
You make visible the
wide blue of your Dutch window,
the sky, which I seldom watch
but know is there. I follow
your track of mud, pale black,
with the rain still shining.

I am blind, and would wake.
Will I ever give up denying
the loathsome laziness in
violent things? The hard,
human labor in your subtle paint;
the lacerate harmonies.

FRANZ SCHUBERT

His father said, "Cut it out, stop writing music,
I can't stand listening to that stuff anymore.
Don't you see there's a world, people, jobs,
                              children,
picnics and a good steady life?
It's not just that you're missing it,
but up to your elbows in ink, or coming
                              home drunk,
you haven't the slightest idea of what's
                              going on.
You never go to funerals, church-meetings,
                              weddings.
I can't stand it, you'll have to get out."

The so-called boy in question
was almost twenty-one. He packed his bags
                              and went,
and never did anything for the rest of his life.

Instead, he sat like a prisoner in his room,
tied down to the piano, as by a chain.
He never stopped working, and was debauched
whenever he did; and always got out too late
to see the sun. But some compulsion,
                    compassion,
made him act like that. Melody, he imagined,
was the only way to breathe.

It was a wild skirmish at the end,
but he died among friends.
However, his father was right, he never knew
how to live. It must have been depressing,
at least for the old man. Schubert barely
                    made it
to thirty-one. Even though later,
who could have known, blob-faced people
                    on picnics

and bunches of little children, heard what
he wrote and thought it fine. *Ave Maria*
was performed at funerals and weddings.
Happy lovers, holding hands, looked satisfied,
as if they had all just tasted a good dish
of sauerkraut.

FOR THE MARKET

It is true, modern life is complicated.
the feedback echoes before it speaks;
the machine, lumping redress, cannot
                        be directed.
Additions radiate into the meaningless,
                        and nothing.

What is left over, but the will to work?
To weave, like an old peasant on a
                        dusty summer day,
rugs of intelligence, berry-dyed lucidities,
to sell to exploiters, and the restless rich.

THE SUBWAY CHURCH

The subway is the church
where all our eyes ride level
comprehending good and evil;
blood squeezed to its extreme.
No false rhetoric, to lead.
But foot-jawed out of hell,
and sharp angels of control
holding back some final
human horror. Each measured
on his own, and the scream
of the tracks is a sermon.
Ancient, flea-bag shy ones
wait their turn; or a criminal
takes command. And heroes must
adroitly turn to secretly be kind.
The soul is stretched beyond
to what suffering cannot mend.

In all eyes we see the truth,
and hold the truth in hand.
Underneath this hard damned earth,
the subway is the church.

ON FIRST HEARING BERLIOZ
IN SARATOGA

    This crop of reality is beyond the
                        new intrusion;
to give of yourself, neither cant,
                        nor calculation;
good health. You are like a small town,
a purpose underpaid, but its own
                        demesne.
As the cicada sings, expressing
an effortless value,
as joy maintains for all
and privacy,

suddenly the gold horn speaks.
Or does it listen?

MOZART

He never saw a tree, they say,
when he rode in his rumbling coach,
peg-seated and easy to lurch,
through the forests of Germany.
He sat with a pad on his knee
and braced himself, head and toe,
and sketched on his rocky way
four quartets and one symphony.

The birds all sang, as he passed,
and featured glissando, their wings;
brooks murmured their musical songs,
but on him, these nice metaphors lost.
No time! only time to be pressed
between measures, the genius too fast.
He made his decision, and placed
three eighth-notes behind a half-rest.

JFK

W<small>HO</small> exposed himself to danger, by doubting
                              power;
the winds are no less inept at identity.
Strands of stoic conscience bid us on,
the movement acquires its business as a gross
innumerable, among the scope of many futures.
But he exposed his life before a butcher.
Time tells, history repeats, nothing explained.
And the useful die young,
                      to flatter cynicism.

MATTER AND REALITY

Anger is the dishonesty,
blunt thong bearing down
on dewdrop and green.
Smashed glass is the escaping
from purling wit and supple truth;
the flat of a hand, and a gun
are the great venomed eyes
of the false and dissembling.
How they leer and call it
"uplift"—matter and reality.
So, the flame of the cool
dies of its pain,
that could have dissolved
all tense conditioned wars,
blocking each from each
for bloody nothing.

W. W. PLAZA

WALT, they have torn down your
                    Brooklyn house,
and build a new plaza with your name.
Do roach-eaten sinews already invade
                    the top story?
Leave out the irony, you will.
Mediocrity fondles with the same
insinuating sickness as in your time.
But you will not have it.
The test is: the poem.
Democracy, not by economic rape
or tacking a name on a building,
but by poetry, your house—
the first élan.

NOVEMBER 1963

To overcome an encumbrance to destiny,
he had to invent a felicity, which meant death.
What was death? a small token of innovation,
a pointless gun made by infinite factions.
Life was a spiral that cuts off sidewise,
mainly by heading you into an enterprise
                                you could
not resist. So he died. And the end ploughed
                                under
was full of mock funerals, and high, historic
                                grumblers,
unctuous as the sport of denigration.
Who mourns? The future. That has not learned
                                to speak.
Christ abides. And only opportunists weep.

THE BUILDER

The builder carries the nails in his cap.
With one hand he uses a hammer,
with the other he props a board.
The scaffold that holds him seems steady.

He has on a red cotton sweater
with a peaked monk's hood;
the material is pink in places
with patches and fading.

He is outside the window
above the fifth floor
of a brownstone being renovated.
His hands and face are brown

like touches of similar dark.
His body leans out over empty spaces.
He is apparently not concerned
with the chance he is taking.

One leg hangs onto a rope,
he bends to pick up a saw.
His foot slides over the wood
like a blind ice-skater.

He is only doing his work.
But that is not the question.
He is so dangerously above the street,
we are afraid at even watching.

The building has new air conditioning;
and will rent for four hundred dollars
     per floor.
The scaffold swings by hooks, dug in
     not to fall.
But worse on a windy day.

GIVERS & TAKERS

Out of your side eye you see them,
the givers and takers, the killers
or sustainers. Quiet at the wheel;
or at the pitch of erratic traffic
some vent their cruelties
in the guise of acceptable accident.
"We can't help that it happened!"
Or, those who helped to avoid.
The generous flinch in the stomach;
or, the eyeball craving blood.

Some men, seeming bloodless as steel,
were shaping the gentle enactment.
Others, oozing good neighbor appeal,
were planning the mordant assault.
Our causes are puzzles in crises.
But, look to veiled wishes in air.
We help, or we hate; we give or we take.
Slice havoc. Or mop up despair.

BEYOND HYSTERIA

Your death brings up subjects
too staunchly, tenderly, believed in
to express to the mob, with its glutted
taste and gun. The credo of devotion
is what they trample on. And men of
good will are the delicacy on which
they suck. Who can tell them, beyond
hysteria, that what they loved was
in the work?

IDEAS ARE FOR USE, NOT SERVITUDE

(In contrast to "Conscience doth make cowards of us all.")

CONSCIENCE must make heroes of us now,
or we are pigs in a trough, slobbering
over our newscasts, accepting like greasy
rinds the stale predictions, from keepers
that keep us lying, prone in mental filth,
swilling down vacuous thoughts (with violence
for dessert). Must we believe what we are
told? because a sociologist says it's so?
that people must turn themselves into swine
and cowards? Immobilized by grief, must we
chomp on the bilge of death? Men need not be
victims of that sloth. Conscience must rout
us out. Misconcepts are not fate. The opaque
truth is choice,
                             and what we make.

IS?

Is the equalization of ideas a slow rot?
It is not. But the temptation to include
the rude and contemptuous takes emphasis
as forthrightness, when it is spite. None-
theless, we share sympathy with the morons
to prove we are fast ones; meanwhile the
verdure spreads on the land; and the good
will gradually win.

THE INSTRUMENT

To be like a pile driver.
And cut through that limbo
of inarticulation,
human rock and mass,
to dense society.
The mob that I'm opposing.
I'll dig it down,
and pound against my years
that waited all the while
pleading for good actions.
I'll gash into that down-bent
root submission.

You concrete lawns and hearts,
I know that you are hard.
But I will strike for bone,
pulse hammer hitting stone.

Nor find the boredom boring,
but think myself like iron,
and justice like a javelin.
Anguish is a good machine;
high-frame for wedge-shaped
charges crashing down.
To break the malice of things.
For sluice of love and change.
Yes, I believe in foundations,
but not as they appear.
The ghosts of what we are,
desire, compressed like steam.
Then the battering, steadfast work;
and clearing ground.

Jane Mayhall's novel *Cousin to Human* was published by Harcourt, Brace & World. Her essays, short stories and poetry have appeared in *The Michigan Quarterly, Epoch, The Nation, Poetry Northwest, Perspective, Partisan Review, Botteghe Oscure* and other periodicals. All the poems in *Givers & Takers* were, with one exception, written this year.

THE EAKINS PRESS
155 East 42 Street   New York, N.Y. 10017